Robert Overby Parallel: 1978–1969

Robert Overby Parallel: 1978–1969

Terry R. Myers
With a memoir by Marty Neumeier

UCLA Hammer Museum
Los Angeles

This catalogue is published on the occasion of the exhibition *Robert Overby: Parallel, 1978–1969*, organized and presented by the UCLA Hammer Museum of Art and Cultural Center, June 25–September 3, 2000.

Robert Overby: Parallel, 1978–1969 is made possible by a generous grant from The Judith Rothschild Foundation and a gift from Maria Hummer and Bob Tuttle. Additional support has been provided by Kenneth L. Freed and by Toyota.

Editor: Karen Jacobson
Designer: Catherine Lorenz
Printed in Germany by Cantz

Library of Congress Cataloging–in–Publication Data
Myers, Terry R.
    Robert Overby : parallel, 1978–1969 / Terry R. Myers.
        p. cm.
"This catalogue is published on the occasion of the exhibition Robert Overby: Parallel, 1978–1969, organized and presented by the UCLA Hammer Museum of Art and Cultural Center, June 25–September 3, 2000"—T.p. verso.
Includes bibliographical references (p.   ).
    ISBN 0–943739–22–5 (hardcover : alk. paper)
    1. Overby, Robert, 1935–1993—Exhibitions. I. Overby, Robert, 1935–1993. II. Title.
    N6537.O96 A4 2000
    709'.2—dc21

                                                                                        00–008917

Contents

Foreword

Robert Overby: Parallel, 1978–1969 is the first museum survey devoted to California artist Robert Overby, and the first exhibition to fully assess this seminal period in Overby's career. From its inception, the exhibition was conceived by guest curator Terry R. Myers as the beginning of the public historical life of Overby's 1970s-era production, a means of opening up the artist's work to serious conversation and debate while introducing audiences to the aesthetic, ideological, and material complexities of this diverse and innovative body of work.

Robert Overby was born in 1935 in Harvey, Illinois. He was awarded scholarships to study at the School of the Art Institute of Chicago, Art Center School in Los Angeles, and the Chouinard Art Institute, also in Los Angeles, where he received his bachelor of arts degree and then became an instructor of advertising design. He established a graphic design studio, working for more than fifty major firms and receiving numerous awards. In the late 1970s he designed a logotype for Toyota that is still in use today. Overby's fine art ranged from geometric abstract paintings in acrylic and oils to nickel- and cadmium-plated resin casts of everyday objects, polyvinyl chloride "stretch" paintings, and the stunning latex rubber casts of architectural details, walls, and rooms for which he is best known. After his premature death from cancer in 1993, interest in Overby's work grew, resulting in several modestly scaled solo exhibitions at galleries in Los Angeles and New York. Until now, however, much of his work has never been publicly exhibited. It is therefore extremely gratifying to be able to present Robert Overby's work to a museum audience for the first time. We are also delighted to accompany this exhibition with a scholarly catalogue, the first monograph to explore Overby's artistic production in depth.

On behalf of the museum and its staff I would like to thank the many individuals who have contributed their time and energies to the success of this exhibition. In particular, we are profoundly grateful to Linda Burnham and the estate of Robert

Overby for generously lending the majority of works in this exhibition. On many occasions, Linda has graciously welcomed us into her home and provided access to Overby's archives. Without Linda's unflagging support and enthusiastic participation, this exhibition simply would not have been possible. Also invaluable has been the participation of the private and institutional lenders to the exhibition, whose names are listed on page 9. We are also extremely grateful to The Judith Rothschild Foundation and to Maria Hummer and Bob Tuttle, whose generous support made the exhibition and its accompanying publication possible. In addition, we owe a debt of gratitude to Kenneth L. Freed and to Toyota for their support of the exhibition. We would also like to extend our special thanks to Ralph Gibson and Steve Kahn, for allowing us to reproduce their photographs in this catalogue, and to Marty Neumeier, for granting us permission to reprint portions of his memoir of Robert Overby. Jessica Fredericks and Andrew Freiser deserve special mention for their assistance with several aspects of the exhibition and catalogue. On behalf of the curator, we would also like to thank Linda Daniels, Steve Kahn, Tom Knechtel, and Karl Petrunak for sharing their memories of Overby.

A number of UCLA Hammer Museum staff members contributed their immense talents to the success of this exhibition. In particular, I would like to thank Claudine Isé, assistant curator, for her able and dedicated management of the exhibition and catalogue, and Cynthia Burlingham, Grunwald Center associate director and senior curator, for overseeing the catalogue's production. James Elaine, curator of contemporary and special projects; Susan Lockhart, registrar of paintings and sculpture; Mitch Browning, chief preparator; Terry Morello, director of external affairs; Marpessa Dawn Outlaw, development associate; and Amy Dove, curatorial assistant, each made invaluable contributions to the project.

In addition, we would like to thank editor Karen Jacobson, whose valuable suggestions helped to refine the catalogue text, and designer Catherine Lorenz, who has produced a volume that reflects the spirit of Robert Overby's work with remarkable sensitivity. Finally, we are tremendously grateful to guest curator Terry R. Myers for organizing *Robert Overby: Parallel, 1978–1969*. Terry's enthusiasm, energy, and commitment—along with his strong, clear, yet nuanced understanding of Robert Overby's work and its importance to the history of California art—have inspired and invigorated us all throughout every stage of this project.

Ann Philbin
Director

Lenders to the Exhibition

Joe Barron
Linda Burnham
Charlotte and Paul Corddry
Kenneth L. Freed
Joe Fronek
Tony and Gail Ganz
Leonard Hirshan
Arlene and Barry Hockfield
Steve Kahn
Jeff Kerns
Tom Knechtel
Tom Lazarus
Marty Neumeier
Estate of Robert Overby
Lari Pittman and Roy Dowell
John Robertshaw
Barry Sloane
Susan and Barry Sussman
Dean Valentine and Amy Adelson
Whitney Museum of American Art
Private collection (3)

Nobody's Paragon
Marty Neumeier

When I was still a promising young graphic designer—all graphic designers are promising when they're young—I had already established a successful studio with a wall full of awards. The pride I felt in my achievements had gone well beyond pride, into the realm of secret embarrassment. How could one young person be so remarkably talented?

One morning at the studio, while working on a Highly Significant Project, my concentration was broken by the familiar *cling-ting* of the front doorbell. I got up from my drawing board and peered around the corner. A homeless man had walked into the reception area and was now riffling through my samples. One tail of faded flannel hung over his dirty white jeans. The knees were torn, and bare toes broke through the tops of his canvas shoes. His face was unshaven, and his hair, cut military-short, stuck out at odd angles.

"Can I help you?" I said, like the proprietor of a china shop.

"This your stuff?" he said.

I nodded.

"Your type's terrible," he said.

I could feel my veneer peeling. "These pieces are national—*inter*national—award winners."

He stared. "So?"

"So," I said, "what's wrong with the type?"

He tilted his head. "Well, just *look* at it."

So began a decade-long relationship between mentor and protégé. Designer-cum-artist Robert Overby . . . Bob . . . later, just Overby . . . forcing me to look at the visual world without blinking. Me wondering what he got out of it.

He'd show up once a week with no warning. We'd have lunch. Afterwards he'd say, "Okay, let's see it," meaning whatever I was working on. Then, shaking his head, "If you're going to do *that*, you'd better take a look at Brodovitch." Or Rand, or Lissitsky, or whoever it was who did it first or did it better.

Sometimes I'd protest: "You hardly even looked at it."

"I have fast eyes," he'd say.

He had to adopt me, because on my own I wouldn't have sought a mentor. And if I had, I wouldn't have chosen Overby. He was nobody's paragon. From what I could tell, he had few friends except for his own mentor, Lou Danziger, whom he often fought with. His personality was a Rand-like contradiction of tough guy and intellectual, and a severe case of rheumatoid arthritis had long ago caused him to dispense with the social niceties.

His critiques were stark and raw and never failed to irritate me. Yet they came from a respect for craft rather than from maliciousness, and from a deep admiration for the world's great designers (who, by implication, were not me). Many years later he would toss me a crumb: "You've become—well—a fairly competent designer."

.   .   .

In the early 1980s he moved south and I moved north, and our friendship (the words *mentor* and *protégé* were never uttered) shifted into maintenance mode. Although I didn't know it, I'd been given a gift few people ever get.

Several years after Overby and I had gone our separate ways, I received news that he had died. After fifty-eight years, his body, weakened by arthritis, had betrayed him one last time. His wife, Linda, called to ask if I would come to Los Angeles and say a few words at the funeral. If I didn't, she worried, nobody would.

When I arrived, I found the chapel overflowing. There were more than a hundred mourners, yet the mood was anything but mournful. It was joyful, even giddy, as we shook hands and marveled at the variety of Overby's acquaintances.

I listened to the service from outside the chapel doors, as dozens of speakers, one after another, pushed their way to the microphone. Even a young man who worked at the car wash got up. He told the story of how, at first, they had only talked about cars. Later they began talking about art. A few weeks ago, the young man said, he had enrolled in art school.

But the real surprise came afterwards at the reception. Everyone I talked to had the same story to tell: each had thought he was Overby's only friend.

This essay is excerpted from "Mentoring," originally published in *Critique*, no. 10 (winter 1999): 27, 37.

Robert Overby
at the door of his
studio at 4540
Hollywood Boulevard,
Los Angeles, 1971.
Photograph by Ralph
Gibson.

Robert Overby
in front of
*Living room,
Paul's place*, 1971.
Photograph by Ralph
Gibson.

Robert Overby during
the casting of *Saulle's
Place*, April 1971.
Photograph by
Steve Kahn.

Plates

1
3 Line Painting
1978
[Cat. no. 67]

2
Monster Blue
1978
[Cat. no. 66]

3
Yellow Frag
1978
[Cat. no. 65]

4
White Grid
1977
[Cat. no. 64]

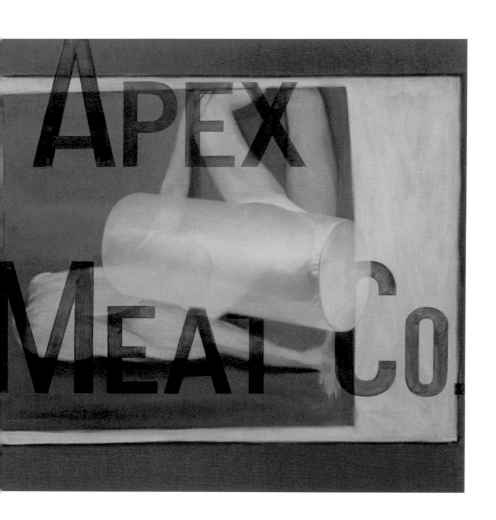

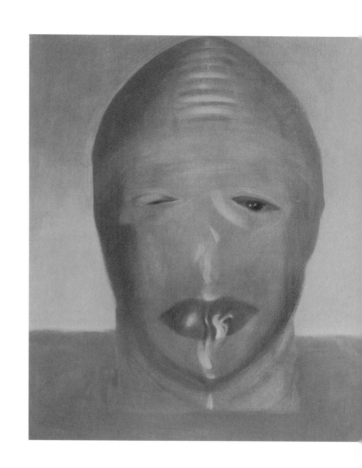

5
Apex Meat
1974–77
[Cat. no. 63]

6
Pink Head
1974–77
[Cat. no. 62]

7
T-Zone
1977
[Cat. no. 61]

8
Black Head
1975
[Cat. no. 59]

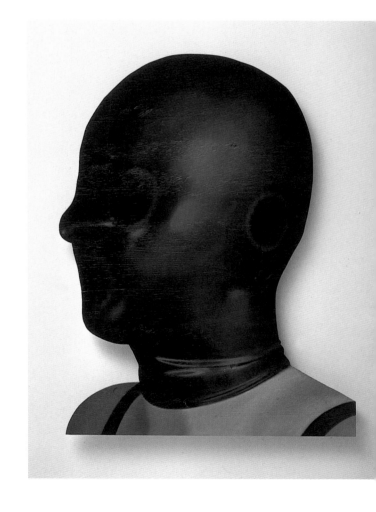

9
Oh Annie
1975
[Cat. no. 58]

10
White wall
with drawing
27 July 1973
[Cat. no. 57]

11
Dürer head on fake
wood panel
15 January 1973
[Cat. no. 55]

12
Sky Plane
28 December 1972
[Cat. no. 54]

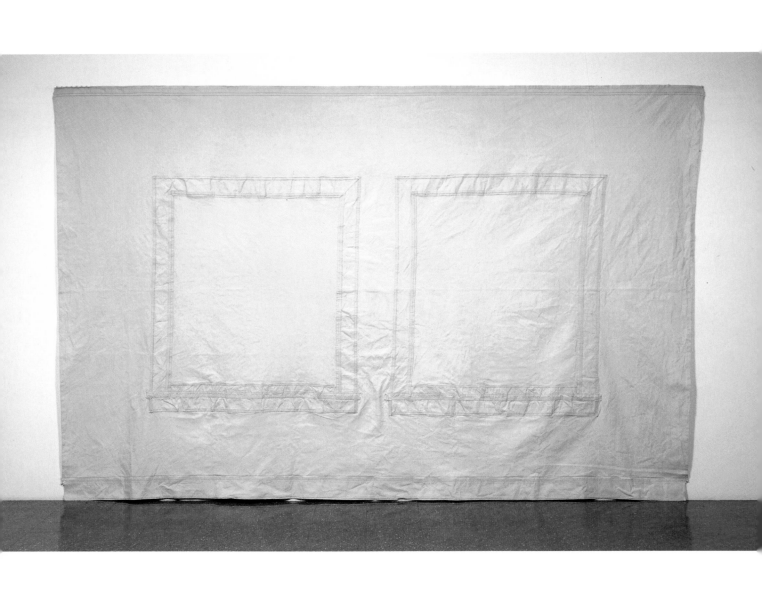

13
Two window wall map
20 August 1972
[Cat. no. 52]

14
Green screen door
10 July 1972
[Cat. no. 48]

15
Corner piece
unlimited multiple
15 June 1972
[Cat. no. 45]

16
Stairwell, Paul's place
29 December 1971
[Cat. no. 44]

17
Living room,
Paul's place
29 December 1971
[Cat. no. 43]

18
Living room,
Paul's place
29 December 1971
[Cat. no. 43]

19
Light meters,
Paul's place
16 December 1971
[Cat. no. 42]

20
Blue door edge
8 April 1971
[Cat. no. 40]

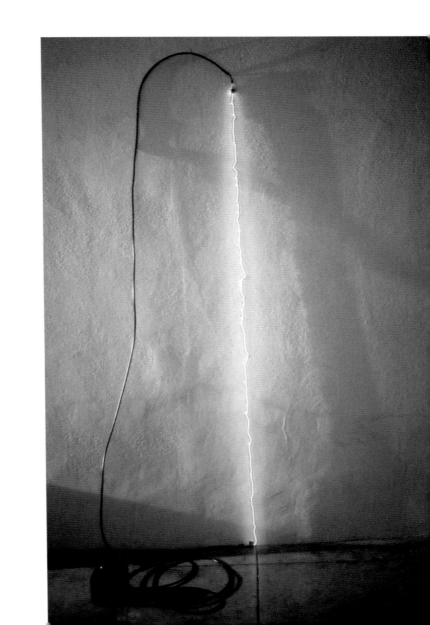

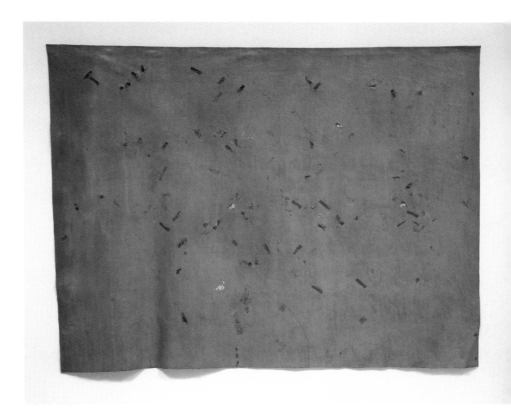

21
Long wall, third floor
4 August 1971
[Cat. no. 38]

22
Scotch tape painting,
third floor
4 August 1971
[Cat. no. 37]

23
East room with
2 windows, third floor
4 August 1971
[Cat. no. 35]

East room with
2 windows, third floor
[detail]

24
Closet doors, third floor
4 August 1971
[Cat. no. 34]

25
*East hall wall, third
floor (Grey wall)*
4 August 1971
[Cat. no. 33]

26
Paul's door, third floor
4 August 1971
[Cat. no. 31]

27
Door without center panel, third floor
4 August 1971
[Cat. no. 30]

28
Installation view,
Burnett Miller Gallery,
Los Angeles, 1995.
From left: *Back of
Garage Door*, 10 July
1972; *Green door with
small window*, 11 July
1972 (cat. no. 49);
*North hall wall, second
floor*, 4 August 1971
(cat. no. 29).

29
*Door with hole,
second floor*
4 August 1971
[Cat. no. 28]

30
Garage Door
13 May 1971
[Cat. no. 24]

31
Blue screen door
11 March 1971
[Cat. no. 23]

32
*Concrete screen
door handle*
20 February 1971
[Cat. no. 22]

33
Opaque door edge
24 February 1971
[Cat. no. 20]

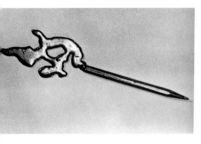

34
R.M. Rill
7 February 1971
[Cat. no. 17]

35
Projected space
between my legs
16 October 1970
[Cat. no. 15]

36
Concrete screen doors
9 October 1970–
22 January 1971
[Cat. no. 14]

Concrete screen doors
[detail]

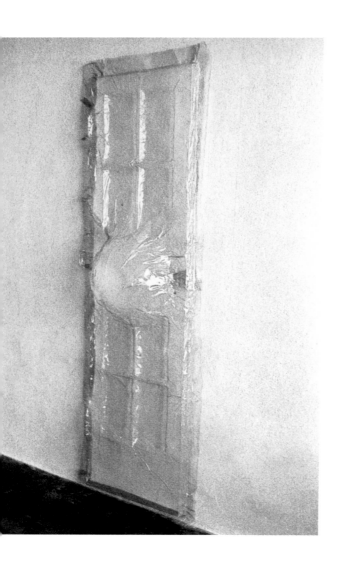

37
Madonna Door
5 October 1970
[Cat. no. 13]

38
Lizard Soup No. 2
20 September 1970
[Cat. no. 12]

39
Plaid No. 4
13 August 1970
Polyvinyl chloride
and resin
119.4 x 146 cm
(47 x 57½ in.)
[Destroyed; not in
exhibition]

40
Sky-Hi
14 July 1970
[Cat. no. 6]

41
Tan and Blue Stretch
8 July 1970
[Cat. no. 5]

42
Adhesium
October 1969
[Cat. no. 4]

Going Overby
Terry R. Myers

The *déjà vu* effect has often been described. . . . But has the counterpart of this temporal removal ever been investigated, the shock with which we come across a gesture or a word as we suddenly find in our house a forgotten glove or reticule? And just as they cause us to surmise a stranger who has been there, there are words or gestures from which we infer that invisible stranger, the future, who left them in our keeping.

Walter Benjamin[1]

Real Time in our culture of the copy is reel-to-reel time. Instant replay begins at birth and continues through second childhood. What we get from the déjà vu is the hint of loss and the prospect of gain; what we take from the replay is collateral and confidence. . . . An art therapist gives residents of a retirement manor Polaroid cameras whose "instant feedback" may produce a "heightened awareness of self." Documenting their environment and the responses of those around them, they see themselves as interactive human beings. A final photographic exercise asks them: "What can you give up and still be you?"

Hillel Schwartz[2]

Given the proliferation of such things as Web cams and the downloadable digital image in current cultural production, it has become all the more critical to look closely at diverse and lesser-known bodies of work from recent history. The late 1960s and 1970s, in particular, demand to be understood as a watershed period during which many artists believed that their investigations of the personal and the political could benefit from the inclusion of the technological. The artwork that Robert Overby produced from 1969 to 1978 exists as meaningful residue of deeply personal investigations of the space between déjà vu and replay, between that sublime feeling that we get when we're not sure if we've experienced something before, and the more self-conscious analysis we're likely to engage in when faced with a more technical "playback." The tension between these moments is what holds Overby's work in a particularly resonant and unusually productive form of suspended animation: the déjà vu "frozen," the playback on a perpetual, "tugging" pause.

The moving effect of this stillness is surely the reason why Overby, unlike many of his peers, never worked in film or video: his interest in things (objects) that are visually "lasting" yet physically fugitive *all at once* seems to have kept him from using time-based media. It is important to recognize that by being the results of a process-driven method of "generational" replication that challenged not only established notions of originality but also the (emotionally loaded) "original" object itself, his resolutely experimental works—whether produced in polyvinyl chloride, latex rubber, neon, or even oil on canvas—were for him most meaningful in terms of how they stood still yet were transformed over time: wear, use, decay, destruction, disappearance. Replaying here the 1967 words of Michael Fried to tell another story, it may very well be that in Overby's works "presentness is grace" precisely because it does *not* exist outside of time.[3] This is what keeps his work fundamentally photographic in nature, a "snapshot" attempting to preserve a prior moment while

accumulating more of its own.

According to Steve Kahn, a photographer and longtime friend, Overby, like Voltaire, strongly believed that everything you needed to make art was "in your backyard."[4] It was of critical importance to him that his work be connected to key people, places, and things in his life.[5] For Overby, like many of the artists working in the 1970s, some of whom were direct influences on him, technology was a tool best used for tending one's own "garden," for cultivating a more expansive, self-critical relationship to work and life that would resist collapsing into (mere) formalism. The uses and abuses of formalism in art production were, of course, major concerns for most of the artists from that time whom we consider significant today. For many of them minimalism was seen as the end of the line. If, as Anna Chave has written, "Minimalism forms the terse, but veracious last word in a narrowly framed argument about what modern art is or should be,"[6] then it should come as no surprise that the art movements that emerged in its wake (postminimalism, *arte povera*, feminist art, conceptualism, etc.) would readily embrace things, techniques, and/or experiences that made room for attempts at infiltration and/or crossover, or "formlessness" and/or the explicitly referential—an openness, it seems now, that was allowed only to a certain degree.

What emerges from the details of Overby's

story is that the inclusion of his work into the "system" (which *almost* happened, as is discussed below) was made difficult for two reasons in particular: he was a very successful and influential graphic designer (full-time from 1960 to 1970 and intermittently afterward), and he didn't "decide to become an artist" until 1969. Given the degree to which artists since the late 1960s have become "professionals," the question does remain about how we should regard these facts today. What is clearer and much more interesting is how much Overby's work speaks to both its and our time in terms of what it is, what it looks like, and what it means.

When it came to looking at, thinking about, and making things, Overby actually had three parallel and equivalent loves: graphic design, model airplanes, and art. The first provided a living, the second related significantly to his childhood and adolescence (as well as being the one thing that could remain private), and the third not only demonstrated how much everything he made was interrelated but also provided him with the best opportunities for using specific content that was important to him, regardless *or precisely because of* any formal or representational similarities that would emerge between his art and that of others. Overby's desire for an everyday connectedness should be kept in mind when we read things like the sketchbook note that he wrote in 1972: "Uniqueness is of no consequence. Anyone can parallel me."[7] The suggestiveness of such a statement precisely echoes the spirit of its time, a period when many believed that what an artwork meant, rather than what it happened to resemble (whether it was another art object or something more commonplace), was the thing that would lead to a certain liberation from such obvious things as the market (whose machinations Overby knew well from his design career) and from other, more complicated aesthetic and ideological structures, like style. What Overby's work demonstrates to this day in the midst of such a hope is how much a willingness to let something look like something else in fact made issues of resemblance *more* rather than less critical.

Sue Spaid—who deserves tremendous credit for bringing Overby's early work to the attention of the 1990s art world by organizing an exhibition at her L.A. gallery in 1994—summed up his work as follows: "Bob's objects were not just things, they were full of intent whether it was to make us see, to characterize some unusual surface, or to see how far he could go with one object (castings, maps, drawings, objects, neon, etc.). All of these 'things' served to extend the life of the original concept or object."[8] Her words remind us that everything in Overby's work that now says "replay" has been amplified by the fact that the work was for the most part not much known

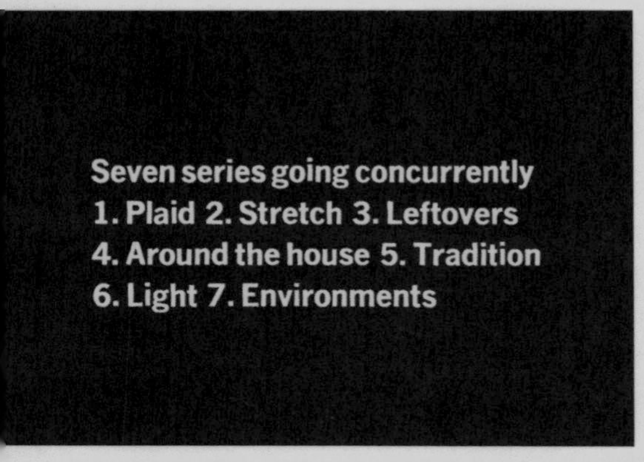

Seven series going concurrently
1. Plaid 2. Stretch 3. Leftovers
4. Around the house 5. Tradition
6. Light 7. Environments

Figure 1
One of the slides from
Overby's slide presentation,
July 1970.

key point here is that the work does not suffer from the "anxiety" of influence either then or now; again, resemblance was always of critical concern, but never a problem.

Today we can speak productively about Overby's work in relation to such things as "sampling." The musical analogy is an apt one in several regards, not only in terms of its connection to design strategies like appropriation (a 1980s term, even if it existed in the 1960s), or to those rather intangible "qualities" that characterize authorship, but also in its temporal nature, resulting from an approach that allows us to be "in" the past and the present simultaneously in "real time"—*parallel*. For Overby, "parallel" was always the point. For example, as early as one year after his decision to become an artist, in slides of descriptive text that he prepared for a presentation of his work, he outlined what he had been doing since the middle of 1969 (fig. 1):

Slide 3:
July to December 1969
Exercises in the following
formal spacial [*sic*] vocabulary

Slide 4:
Atmospheric illusion
Overlapping planes

during its time; several of the works in this exhibition are being shown for the first time. The invocation of Benjamin's "stranger" at the beginning of this text— the future in our present—serves a purpose here, as "his" presence is felt in the *domestic* aspects of artwork beginning its public life after the premature death of its maker. (Overby died at the age of fifty-eight of Hodgkin's disease after fighting severe arthritis throughout much of his adult life.) Retrospectives are by definition fraught with opportunities for the déjà vu and/or replay effect. In this case, given what the work is, and who Overby was, this effect is all the more present, particularly when the work appears to have been influential when there was no way it could have been—for example, in the 1990s work of Tim Hawkinson, Glen Seator, and Rachel Whiteread.[9] The

Perspective illusion
Emperical [*sic*] logic

Slide 5:
January to July 1970
Major concern to delineate and
transcribe the aspects of time

Slide 7:
Seven series going concurrently
1. Plaid 2. Stretch 3. Leftovers
4. Around the house 5. Tradition
6. Light 7. Environments[10]

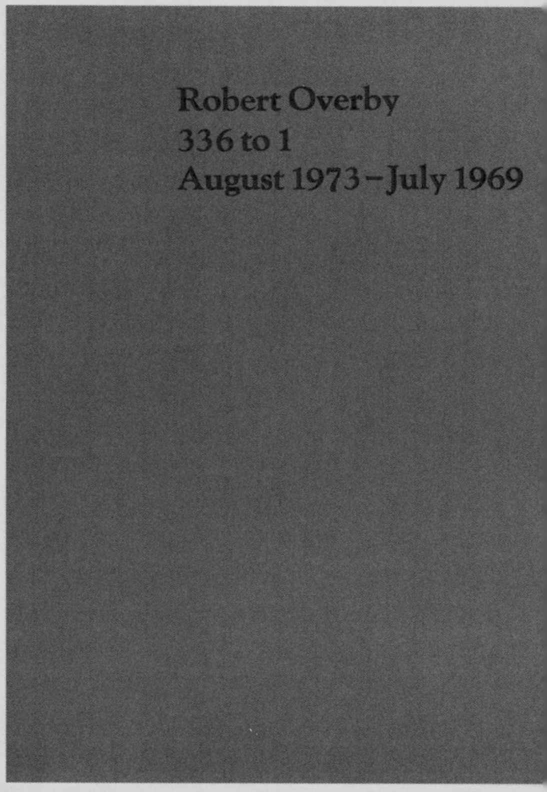

A few years later Overby would provide
even stronger evidence of his commitment to the parallel. In 1974, two and a half years after suffering a
series of career setbacks that will be discussed below,
he self-published a small red paperback book called
Robert Overby: 336 to 1, August 1973–July 1969 (fig.
2). In it he documented every artwork that he made
during its four-year time span in reverse chronological order, in most cases down to the actual day that
they were completed. It is not hyperbole to suggest
that the so-called red book rescued Overby's artwork
from oblivion. Moreover, for those of us who are com-
ing to the work after the fact, it proves by showing
rather than telling us that nothing Overby ever did

Figure 2
Overby's "red book,"
Robert Overby: 336 to 1,
August 1973–July 1969
(height: 15.9 cm [6 1/4 in.]).

**Robert Overby
336 to 1
August 1973 – July 1969**

would ever be best understood in isolation.

David Rimanelli's realization of the book's
implications, recounted in his insightful review of
what would be Overby's first New York solo exhibition, at Jessica Fredericks Gallery in November 1996

Figure 3
Installation view of
Robert Overby, 1971–1985, at
Jessica Fredericks Gallery,
New York, November 30,
1996–January 12, 1997.
From left:
*Kitchen cabinets, Paul's place,
12 December 1971*; *What else is
important*, 1981.

recalling Frank Stella's "Protractor" and "Polish Village" paintings. Incidentally, these early works have obvious similarities to graphic design, the field in which Overby excelled.[11]

It is reasonably clear that Overby organized his book in reverse chronological order not only to lead a reader/viewer back to his start in graphic design (a goal that seems to be reinforced by the singular inclusion of an offset lithograph identified as *The Film and Modern Art poster*, which announces an October 1969 exhibition at the Municipal Art Gallery in L.A.'s Barnsdall Park) but also to emphasize once again that his fundamental concern was with the ways in which he—like all people, places, and things—moved through, and changed over, time.

.   .   .

(fig. 3), is telling. While attempting to reconcile the two main bodies of work included in the show—the latex casts and the representational paintings—he picks up the book:

> After looking at a copy, one realizes that the apparent dichotomy in the present show is just the tip of the iceberg: no, it's not a question of two competing styles, but maybe ten, twenty styles, all of which the artist worked in at more or less the same time. Alongside avant-gardist experiments, there are painterly pastiches after the old masters. Process art and Pop art, Nauman, Keith Sonnier, Eva Hesse, Robert Ryman, Richard Serra, etc. Andy Warhol and Claes Oldenburg. . . . The earliest works are acrylic paintings, some on shaped canvases,

A lot of designers are hung up on innovation. I shoot for a non-faddish image, but I'm not really looking to innovate. I find if you stick to the problem, are accurate in your analysis of it, you're going to come out with unique solutions at the other end. True innovation is somehow after the fact: you can only see it from a histori-cal viewpoint.

Robert Overby, 1979[12]

In 1969 Overby was hired to buy "art" for the CBS Studio Center in Studio City, California. His employer was Louis Dorfsman, vice president of advertising and design for the CBS Broadcasting Group in New York, who confirmed the deal in a letter to Overby dated July 1:

> For starters, it was good to meet with you at last. That evening with Lou Danziger was most pleasant. Too bad my "staying power" wasn't what it should have been. Sorry I cut out so early.
>
> This note is meant as a confirmation of our verbal agreement that you accept the chore of acquiring 300 or more, as needed, pieces of "art" for CBS Studio Center structure.
>
> As we discussed, at a propitious time you must visit there to get a "feel" for the building and at that time I'll arrange for your introduction to Gordon Stulberg, President, so you can get that "feel" also. He may have very definite ideas about his own office. I think we covered the subject of interior "ART" rather well during our day together. We certainly seemed to be on a similar frequency in terms of taste, style, ideas, improvisation, gimmicks, shticks, etc. We can operate from both coasts hopefully without stumbling over each other but rather being helpful to each other.[13]

The 288-piece collection that Overby ultimately assembled for the CBS Studio Center building takes inclusiveness to the extreme in terms of both style (historical, contemporary) and substance (media, function, etc.), incorporating everything from mass-produced images of art (for example, Matisse and Picasso bookplates; posters of the Venus de Milo and Andrew Wyeth's *Christina's World*); to contemporary art in several forms (lithographs and serigraphs by Ellsworth Kelly, Nicholas Krushenick, Sister Corita Kent, and Nobuyuki Hadeisihi; two very early [and unusual] abstract geometric paintings—*Lopeshore* and *Temple Street*—by Allen Ruppersberg; a Plexiglas box construction that Overby commissioned from Charles Arnoldi;[14] black-and-white photographs by friends Steve Kahn and Ralph Gibson); to examples of "craft" (three Navajo rugs and two genuine circuit boards acquired from Lockheed Electronics at no cost).[15] It comes as no surprise, given the broad context, that Overby included one example of his graphic design, a poster for a futurism exhibition. What is quite surprising, however, is that he also included seventeen of his own works of *fine* art.

Before we get to Overby's momentous decision in 1969 to switch gears and become a fine artist,

David Smith   a memorial exhibition

Figure 4
Catalogue for *David Smith:
A Memorial Exhibition,*
Los Angeles County Museum
of Art, November 3, 1965–
January 30, 1966 (designed by
Robert Overby).

Chaffee in Arkansas. Afterward he moved to Los Angeles to attend Art Center School (before it moved to Pasadena and became Art Center College of Design) in 1958–59. He was a fellow design student at Art Center with Dick Bell, who in 1969 was the local CBS art director and recommended him for the art-buying job.[16] When Overby accepted it, he was slightly less than a year away from finally receiving a college degree at the age of thirty-four, a B.A. in fine art from Chouinard Art Institute in Los Angeles, where he taught graphics in 1967–68 and again in 1970–71.

Dorfsman's mention in his letter of Lou Danziger is a reference not only to an important colleague in the design world but also to Overby's mentor at Art Center. (Danziger is himself a "descendant" of Paul Rand.) Overby did freelance design work for Danziger while he was his student, and he continued to work for him on occasion even after he had established his own design practice. In the ten years between 1960 and 1970 Overby produced institutional and consumer advertising for more than twenty-five major firms and institutions—including Boeing, CBS, Capitol Records, Container Corporation of America, Ekco-Alcoa, IBM, Los Angeles County Museum of Art (fig. 4), MGM, Schweppes, and Upjohn—and received numerous awards from organizations such as the Seattle Art

it is helpful to know some of his biography. Born in Harvey, Illinois, on May 24, 1935, he moved frequently during his childhood, usually to various suburbs of Chicago (the home base of United Airlines, where his father worked his way up from mechanic to pilot), but also to Seattle for some time. He attended the School of the Art Institute of Chicago in 1953–54 and 1956–57, serving in the army in the interim at Fort

Directors Society, the Art Directors Club of Los Angeles, *Communication Arts* magazine, the American Institute of Graphic Arts, the Society of Typographical Arts, the Type Directors Club of New York, and the Western Association of Art Museums. After 1970 he would take on the occasional design job, most notably in 1977, when he designed a logotype for Toyota that is still in use (fig. 5).

Needless to say, the CBS job was one of those truly life-changing experiences:

> It literally started me, because I could not buy the sized pieces I needed for the budget I had, and there was no slack from New York. . . . So I talked to Dorfsman and said "look, I am really interested in this and I think I can do as well as anybody can doing this, so I am going to start painting some of the paintings," and I did. I painted a whole bunch of paintings. That is why all that early stuff CBS owns . . . because I painted the paintings and sold them to them for cheap prices, basically. It was sixteen times the job for the fee that I got for it. I did it mostly because I was interested in it. And that is how I started painting. . . . I started learning all of this stuff, and then I had huge notebooks of notes, studies, and . . . materials, and I painted in my garage.[17]

Although Overby had studied painting briefly in the mid-1950s at the School of the Art Institute of

Figure 5
TOYOTA: The Authorized Logotype, October 1977. © Toyota Motor Sales, U.S.A., Inc., 1977. Reprinted with permission. Toyota is a registered trademark of Toyota Motor Corporation.

Chicago, he never pursued it professionally until 1969. A quick glance at the first paintings that he made for CBS—several of which were also shown in his first solo exhibition, which took place in December 1969 at the Chouinard Gallery (fig. 6)—reveals that he was reacting to the type of formal maneuvers that had defined much American painting

Figure 6
Installation view of Overby's
exhibition at Chouinard
Gallery, Los Angeles, December
1969. From left: *Football, Blue
Sink, Right Turn Only (RTO),
Cubist Sink*, all December 1969.

of the 1960s. He would later acknowledge that they were too indebted to Frank Stella: "I was treading the same ground, doing the same experiments and why waste my time."[18] Likewise, many of Overby's earliest works are also directly connected to the logotype and trademark design for which he had become rather well known. The serigraphs that he also produced at the time (many of which were also sold to CBS) clearly indicate in their deliberate diversity—in terms of form, style, and subject matter—that one of his main concerns was to resist developing a signature style in art or design. A work like *Space No. 9 (study for RTO)*, August 1969, for example, literally equates the formal "turns" of a Stella-type shape with a super-graphic symbol for "right turn only," while *Adhesium*, October 1969 (pl. 42), literally "sticks" a self-con-

scious nostalgia for earlier advertising design next to a gestural silver brush stroke. Such art-versus-design juxtapositions didn't hold Overby's interest for long, most likely because they didn't "move" enough.

While doing his "exercises in formal spatial vocabulary" and teaching himself how to paint, Overby was also exploring the image of a "tone bar," a strip or stripe that changes tone across its surface. For him it was not only a "transitional" object that could be moved from design to art but also something that could symbolically represent changing condi-tions: "The tone bar is the synthesis of an idea. . . . Changing tones are the same as blending flesh or any-thing else where there is an imperceptible change. It always fascinates me, and it is the function of life. . . . [It] can be a time line."[19] Overby used it throughout his work, from the very first paintings—like *Space No. 1*, July 1969 (the first work in his red book), in which a diagonal tone bar "moves" from yellow to blue, or the more Stella-like *Cubist Sink*, December 1969 (fig. 6), where the canvas is actually in the shape of two intersecting bars, one of which has a surface that moves almost atmospherically "through" red, yellow, and orange—to later works like *Tone-bar room with 2 doors, first floor*, 4 August 1971 (one of the latex wall castings from the dramatic Barclay House Series), or *Tone-bar door map*, 21 August 1972 (fig. 7). The tone bar is best understood as Overby's first "inclusive" form, one that was simple, surface-oriented, and "all-at-once" in its motionless presence as a shape and image yet, conversely, capable of indicating process, change, and even the passage of time.

 After completing the CBS job, Overby moved away from painting and began to make much more experimental work, manipulating materials—rather than an image like the tone bar—to visually and literally "freeze" a moment in time. Like many of the artists who are now called postminimalists, Overby believed at the time that meaning could be found in the residual visual impact of a particular process, in his case, *stretching*. Such a physical activity was significant for him because it was something "done in human terms—showing human action,"[20] an interpretation supported by the fact that he began his experiments by stretching clothing, in particular handkerchiefs and socks that usually belonged to others. (There is a funny sketch in his notebook of a clothesline on which several of his diverse artworks would be hung.)[21] He also produced several "tests" in which a clear sheet of polyvinyl chloride (PVC) was wrapped around an object—for example, a clothespin or a Coke bottle—and then stretched so that it looked as if the object was moving "in time" against and/or through the PVC, almost as if it were air or water. (In the red book there is a photograph of one that has been made to appear as if a Coke bottle created some

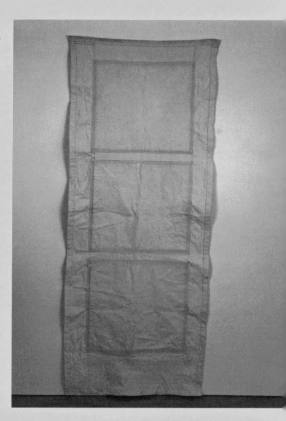

Figure 7
Tone-bar door map
21 August 1972
[cat. no. 53]

sort of "trail" after it lifted off from the floor. Suggestively called *About When*, 6 June 1970, it—like the majority of the PVC work—no longer exists.) From these tests, Overby then began to work with larger sheets of PVC, which he would color with bright resin. After heating one up, he (with occasional help) would then pull it into a particularly "active" position, holding it in place until it was cool enough to hold the "evidence" of what was done to it. For example, *Tan and Blue Stretch*, 8 July 1970 (pl. 41), was crumpled along its diagonal, while *Large Yellow and Silver Stretch*, 16 July 1970, was apparently given several "allover" tugs across its surface, some of which appear to have been done against something (a block of wood?) that was placed behind the upper right corner during the procedure.

Judging from his notes from the time, it's possible that Overby felt that the "frozen motion" of the stretches didn't go far enough: "Stretch shows displacement and tension. Sort of a half-joke—only see where something's been?" Such a question is a reminder here that he would never be completely satisfied with process in and of itself, its particular "human action" was only part of the story; his prior interest in representation and the image would not disappear. Other PVC works that Overby produced at the same time incorporate very particular representational (to some extent even photographic) subject matter, images that have a relationship to the concept of material rather than its physicality. Using actual scraps of fabric as a guide, he created an extensive series of "plaids" (none of which has survived [see pl. 39]) in which he very carefully sprayed vari-

ous colored resins through a metal grid onto a sheet of PVC, mimicking the look of a plaid created by some type of photomechanical printing process. Another idiosyncratic work, *Sky-Hi*, 14 July 1970 (pl. 40), looks as if it were a photographic reproduction of a cloudy sky, a significant image for an artist so enthralled by flight and motion.

Overby's notes from July 29, 1970, are telling, written two weeks after completing *Sky-Hi*: "Hang up—formalizing is getting away from direct experience. How do I institute the emotion? *The feeling?* Stretch was originally intended to satisfy above. Does it? . . . How do you sustain the necessary feeling long enough? Can't do it by showing object—has to be more direct!" It is crucial to note here that the thing that Overby was demanding be more direct was not the object or the process (as would be the case in minimalism or postminimalism), but the *feeling*. In this regard it is not too far-fetched to suggest that his intentions have much in common with the investigations of personal subjectivity that characterized the feminist art of the period—yet another example of the interesting, even challenging connections that Overby's work makes within the matrix of art production during the 1970s.[22]

Along with the stretches and the plaids, in 1970–71 Overby was also making numerous drawings and watercolors (selections from his *50 painting*

sketches, 18 April 1970–16 November 1972, are
included in this exhibition), a few experimental light
sculptures (with punning titles like *Arnoldi's Shine*,
Yellow Scoot, and *Dead of Night*, all 12 July 1970), and
several works that seem to have very personal sources
(for example, an unusual work called *Drew's 'Nam
jungle jumpers fit me, too*, 6 September 1970 [named
after a student of his who went to Vietnam twice],
which contains an actual pair of army pants as well as
Overby's army serial number). Taken in its entirety,
the overwhelming amount of work that Overby produced during this period reveals a strange mixture of
naïveté and sophistication, something of which he
was very well aware, given that, as he put it, he was
"doing things at 35 that others did in their 20s."[23]
Even so, the level to which he was "cranking things
out while catching up" allowed him to make some
very funny work—derivative, of course, but in a sort
of "so what?" fashion. For example, several "Dada"
objects—including *Trilobite*, *Monkey Grip* (fig. 8),
Lizard Soup No. 2 (pl. 38), all 20 September 1970,
and *R.M. Rill*, 7 February 1971 (pl. 34)—make various visual-verbal puns about the "gaps" between what
they're made out of and what they might mean, while
paying appropriate homage to the likes of Marcel
Duchamp, René Magritte, Jasper Johns, and Andy
Warhol. Like many artists of the period, Overby was
heavily influenced by Duchamp (it was Ralph Gibson

Figure 8
Monkey Grip
20 September 1970
[cat. no. 11]

who talked Overby into buying Arturo Schwarz's big
book on Duchamp in a Hollywood bookstore): "Now
my realizations were nowhere as good as Duchamp's
because he spent time fussing and I was just busting
along, you know, trying to get ideas down."[24]

Surely Overby got the joke of what he was
doing when, right after the "Dada" objects, he started
to make things out of concrete, a material that would
make his work (temporarily) more "concrete," slowing it down, if you will, yet still providing opportunities for experimenting with process. Clearly
influenced by Bruce Nauman (the work usually cited
in the recent press on Overby is Nauman's *Cast of the
Space under My Chair*, 1966–68, but there are also

Figure 9
Richard Serra
(American, born 1939)
Doors, 1966–67
Rubber and fiberglass
Four pieces, 91.4 x 274.3 cm
(36 x 108 in.) each;
91.4 x 579.1 cm (36 x 228 in.)
overall
San Francisco Museum of
Modern Art. Fractional gift of
Doris and Donald Fisher

others, like *Six Inches of My Knee Extended to Six Feet*, 1967), he started with his own body, making a work called *Projected space between my legs*, 16 October 1970 (pl. 35). In true Overby fashion, the work had a double relationship to time: first, in the sense that "projected" (i.e., extended, extruded, pulled, stretched) space could represent, like the tone bar, duration, and, second, in that the installation of the piece itself would incorporate a change over time—it was meant to be set into the ground so that grass would ultimately grow over it.

At the same time that Overby introduced concrete into his repertoire of materials, he also found his second significant form: a door. Unlike the tone bar, a door was an everyday object that provided a type of "seen-but-not-known" image: when do we

really *look* at one? Moreover, for Overby a door simultaneously symbolized "human action" and human *presence*, as he told Peter Clothier in 1986: "I see the door definitely as a body. There's no doubt about that. But the door's also something that you set your scale by. I don't know if you've ever been in a house and hit your head on the door but it's really an odd feeling. It's also a barrier—I have that kind of peeping Tom mentality you know, wanting to know what's behind it."[25] Given such burgeoning potential, can it be an accident that the first door, called *Madonna Door*, 5 October 1970 (pl. 37), is literally pregnant with possibilities? Cast in transparent PVC from an old door from which some of the glass windowpanes had been removed to make room for a PVC and resin "belly," it is an ethereal, ghostlike yet, with its many wrinkles and folds, blatantly substantive image, even when juxtaposed with an almost oxymoronic series of concrete *screen* doors (and parts of doors) that Overby cast at the same time: *Concrete screen doors*, 9 October 1970 to 22 January 1971 (pl. 36); *Concrete screen door with hole*; and *Concrete screen door handle* (pl. 32), both 20 February 1971. These were doors to be looked at, not through. Moreover—unlike earlier works such as Richard Serra's *Doors*, 1966–67 (fig. 9), which is made of rubber and fiberglass, like some of Overby's subsequent doors, but tipped on its side in order to force a formal reading—they are still very much to be looked at as *doors*.

More minimal works like *Door edge*, 19 February 1971, and *Opaque door edge*, 24 February 1971 (pl. 33), benefited structurally from the addition of fiberglass to Overby's materials list, as did *Blue screen door*, 11 March 1971 (pl. 31), which stands out not only because of its color but also because of its jagged right edge. *Blue door edge*, 8 April 1971 (pl. 20), is a "drawing" of the same edge in neon, about which Michael Duncan has appropriately remarked: "This glowing work recalls the door's violent transformation in an almost celebratory way—a neon commemoration of an arbitrary yet oddly poignant event."[26] Overby's finding the door could not have come at a better time; it can be argued that it literally "unlocked" his work, releasing it from the grip of self-referential formalism or process and moving it into the vernacular, even domestic places where he felt most comfortable. On the brink of what would be his most productive time, Overby was still missing the one thing that would give him what he needed to make the work simultaneously commemorative and transformative, past *and* present: the perfect medium. He would find it in rubber.

.　　.　　.

One of my goals is to narrow the "reality" gap. Question begged as why not use object as it exists? . . . Answer—actual object (thing taken from) does not usually convey overstatement necessary for communication.

Robert Overby, 1 July 1972[27]

It all began with a pair of socks. On August 1, 1970, Overby finished a couple of drawings of his then-girlfriend's socks—*Stephanie's Sox*, and *Stephanie's Sox are Blue*. In the first, the socks are drawn as if active, alive; in the second, they droop in the most maudlin of ways. A year and a half later, while he was working on the first concrete, resin, and fiberglass doors, he cast a series of socks in wax (*Falling Sock*, *Rauschenberg Sock*, *Fish Sock*, *Reptile Sock*, *Dual Sock*, *Drip Sock*, all 14–18 February 1971). At the same time, he made another sock, *Rubber Sock*, 18 February 1971. Realizing that he had made a major breakthrough in his casting process, he changed his immediate plans: "may postpone painting for major casting projects before Saulle leaves for Israel in April."[28] (The red book confirms that he made no paintings at this time.) Overby had good reason to put his plans on hold: Saulle was helping him make his molds for the door castings, and Overby had found a material that would allow him to make an incredible leap in both the size and the scale of his work.

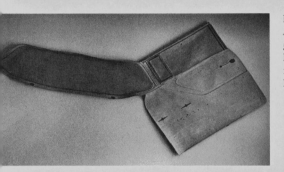

Figure 10
Indian Chief
5 May 1971
Latex rubber
154.9 x 302.3 cm (61 x 119 in.)
Estate of Robert Overby

What was Overby thinking when he decided that his first substantial project in latex rubber would be to cast the entire façade of Saulle's building? One thing we do have is Overby's description of the process:

> Yeah, the latex is painted on. There is some preparatory work—all the undercuts and stuff have to be taken care of, and how you do it is quite laborious. I had a couple of hundred pounds of modeling clay, and I would go around and put it on the back of all of the window frames, and that all had to be filled in, so that none of the rubber goes in back of something because then you can't pull it off. It is just like any other mold, you have to be able to release it. . . . Everything has to be prepared, and then the surface is prepared. You can either shellac the surface, or you can do a number of things to either pull—for instance, this place is an old building, and it had . . . paint that was coming off, and we whitewashed part of it, so that when we put the latex on it, it takes the whitewash off of it. What you are seeing there is powder, because as the rubber comes off, it is very sticky. . . . There are a whole bunch of ways to prepare in stages for what you want. You can put paint on the surface that you want to peel off. You can put pigment in the latex as you do different layers. You can change colors, and it gives you kind of translucent skin-like effects, with warms and cools, and all those sorts of things.[29]

The resulting work, called *Saulle's Place*, 23 April 1971, is fifty feet long, which was surely large enough to convince Overby that he was onto something monumental, not only in physical but also in conceptual terms. Unforgiving in its ability to reproduce detail, latex rubber would "record" far more faithfully than concrete or resin ever could; moreover, it would begin to change as soon as it was completed—in other words, the work quite possibly would never be truly "finished" until it disappeared. (Responding in July 1972 to a letter from an artist asking for advice about using latex, Overby was helpful yet also wrote back, "Preservation of my own work is of secondary consideration.")[30]

Returning temporarily to a more manageable size, Overby then cast three very distinct works. *Lola*, 2 May 1971, was a cast of a human model that was subsequently hung on the wall like a flayed skin (see fig. 12); *Indian Chief*, 5 May 1971 (fig. 10), was taken from the front window and door of an automobile; and *Garage Door*, 13 May 1971 (pl. 30), was a return to the door, albeit a particularly "expressive" one. Clearly buoyed by his success, Overby was beginning to think about showing the work. In January 1971 he made reference in his notes to a possible show at Cirrus, an exhibition that took place at the end of what would prove to be the most productive year of his career. The two works included in that exhibition—*Across the Street*, 14 May 1971, and *Around the House*, 16 May 1971—were done at and, in the case of the latter, on Overby's home on Clinton Street in Los Angeles. The first was a ten-foot-wide latex cast of the width of the street in front of his house (fig. 11); the second, a three-foot-wide and two-hundred-foot-long strip of latex cast of the perimeter of his home. Writing in the *Los Angeles Times*, William Wilson summed up Overby's achievement: "Here is a refreshing addition to the art of printmaking, an especially adept blend of formal abstraction and a sentimental naturalism often found in concept art. It is certainly safe to add Overby's name to a seemingly ungovernable list of gifted new artists here-

Figure 11
View of *Across the street*,
14 May 1971,
draped across two Volkswagen
Beetles after being cast.

abouts."[31] At the end of 1971 it surely did seem safe; Overby's career as an artist was soon to be launched.

Six months prior, right after completing *Across the Street* and *Around the House*, Overby made a fateful six-week trip to New York, staying in a borrowed loft above Ralph Gibson on West Broadway. He had been doing the kinds of things that young artists do to get noticed—for example, sending Leo Castelli a picture a day for almost a month of the work he was doing at the time[32]—and it is clear that the goal of the trip was to get a gallery. (Subsequently he did meet Castelli, who was encouraging.) Even so, Overby also made some significant work while he was there, casting various parts of Gibson's loft—the heavy metal front door, done very thinly, with only a few coats of latex; the window, which in the red book photograph sags in classic Oldenburgian fashion; and, most

Figure 12
Several of Overby's works—
including *15°*, 2 June 1971
(cat. no. 25; foreground);
Ralph's Door, 4 June 1971; and
Lola, 2 May 1971—installed in
Ralph Gibson's New York loft,
June 1971.

that he completed in New York to be "more conceptu-al." *15°*, for example, seems to be moving in two directions at the same time—parallel paths that have been visually twisted ("indexical," some would say) by casting one of the strips at a slight angle to the grid of the bricks.

Overby left New York in mid-June not only with a gallery—John Weber—but also with a solo exhi-bition scheduled for January 1972. As soon as he returned to L.A., he shipped Weber several pieces, and not long after he also had a commitment from Lucio Amelio (who learned about the work when Weber brought several pieces to Europe)[33] to do a solo show at Modern Art Agency Gallery in Naples in November 1971, at the same time as his show at Cirrus—the only show that would actually happen.[34]

. . .

You notice that the surface of metaphor begins to break down. The metaphor of surface becomes the surface of metaphor; the relation among signifiers, posited as a material and his-torical relation, nevertheless continues to be haunted by the deferred ontology that is its point of origin. What has been suppressed is the alterity that will erupt as nature and death—the alterity of the Real. As in the figuration/

unusually, various sections of the brick walls: long vertical strips from a corner, a small rectangular sec-tion that he called a "painting," and *15°*, 2 June 1971 (fig. 12), two room-length strips that run parallel to each other on the floor. Overby considered the work disfiguration of Piranesi, what seems to be noise turns into a cry, what seems to be nature becomes a matter of history.

Susan Stewart[35]

It is not surprising that Overby would return to L.A. after the success he had in New York, get his first real studio (at 4540 Hollywood Boulevard, where it intersects Sunset Boulevard), and immediately produce what is arguably the most significant work of his career: twenty-eight latex casts completed on August 4, 1971, collectively known as the Barclay House Series. That this poignant "body" of work would in retrospect stand to some extent as a literal, even perverse prefiguring of things falling apart is, of course, not the point. Overby was looking for what he called "the overstatement necessary for communication," and the Barclay house—a recently burned and abandoned building near the intersection of the Hollywood Freeway and Melrose Avenue—provided him with an enormous amount of emotionally charged and literally "raw" material. With the help of several others, including his younger brother Paul, Overby made castings from numerous walls, doors, windows, as well as details like a cabinet and a drawer front, most of which were named for their original location in the building: for example, *North hall wall, second floor* (pl. 28); *East hall wall, third floor (Grey wall)* (pl. 25); *Closet doors, third floor* (pl. 24); *East room with 2 windows, third floor* (pl. 23).

So extensive was the damage to the Barclay house that the casting process was transformed from one of documentation and commemoration to one of reclamation and even a strange type of resurrection: when pulled, many of the casts took away substantial amounts of charred wood and paint, even things like telephone wire and tape (found on *Scotch tape painting, third floor* [pl. 22], one of five in the series that Overby defined as "paintings"). Several works—*Paul's door, third floor* (pl. 26); *Door without center panel, third floor* (pl. 27); and *South door, third floor*—are eerily shroudlike, a reading that Overby reinforced by adding black pigment to the latex before applying it to the surfaces. Such an intervention complicates the works' relationship to decay, as David Rimanelli has suggested: "Unlike the entropic dimension to Nauman's work . . . decay functions in Overby's casts in a way at once more literal and more fictional. They simultaneously record decay and represent it. Traces of the ruined original persist, but he could not resist tarting them up as images of ruin. Hence, the whiff of melodrama that clings to these pieces."[36] For Overby, the threat of sentimentality (not to mention the physical decay of the casts themselves) was a risk worth weathering, not only to achieve the "overstatement" that he was looking for but also, as always, to firmly

Figure 13
Stairwell, Paul's place
29 December 1971
[cat. no. 44; pl. 16]

situate the work in the past, present, and future.

Notes in Overby's sketchbook indicate that he was planning to show selections from the Barclay House Series in his November show in Italy.[37] Anticipating the New York show that was to take

place in January 1972, he began work in the fall of 1971 on several major pieces, using his brother's place in Venice. Moving beyond the "melodrama" inherent in the Barclay House Series, these works suggest that Overby was concerned with communicating more than just sentiment: humor was equally important. *Living room, Paul's place*, 29 December 1971 (pls. 17, 18)—Overby's first three-dimensional latex cast—is a mind-bender, "the outside of the inside of the room," as he put it.[38] More than being merely "tarted up," the details of the room have been completely *redone* in a pop fashion: doorways and windows, a wall heater, and even a small "painting" of a flower were "colored in" during the casting process. Compared to the equally impressive yet monochromatic "pure" latex companion work—*Stairwell, Paul's place*, 29 December 1971 (fig. 13, pl. 16)—this living room borders on camp. The humor (among other things) would prove to be a problem.

One of the works that Overby made in New York—*Manhole cover*, 28 June 1971—was shown at John Weber in a late November group show of gallery artists: Carl Andre, Dan Flavin, Richard Haas, Dale Henry, Jeffrey Lew, Sol LeWitt, Robert Ryman, Fred Sandback, Robert Smithson, and Kenneth Snelson. It, along with the rest of Overby's work, was not well received by some of the other artists, and Weber was pressured to cancel his solo show, sending a letter to that effect on December 15.[39] Much could be said about the implications of such resistance, particularly in relationship to our historical understanding of the "openness" of art production at the time, but it is interesting to read what Overby had to say about the situation in 1986: "If I had been in New York then I may have had some say in the matter. . . . But they were right. The problem is that they were right. The work I was doing was not philosophically the same as the gallery artists' work. They had a perfect right to be resistant to it. . . . The only thing about [the work] was that it was conceptual. Otherwise, it was representational, it was photographic, it was like print, it was funny in a way, you know, humorous. It was talking about another kind of reality. You know, they were basically abstract painters."[40]

A June 1972 letter from the artist Robert Kushner provides a different but equally intriguing reaction to Overby's work from the time: "The thing that really wiped me out is the variety and sensuousness of the surfaces. I think of them as lifesize photographs, and the idea of the painter participating in a chemical process that yields a concrete image is what I mean by the conceptual aspects."[41] It's no accident that Kushner used the word *painter*; Overby considered himself one all along—but not (ever) an abstract one.

With terrible timing, the other shoe

dropped on Overby's career. In a letter of November 3, 1971, Lucio Amelio informed Overby that he would have to move his show back because a Joseph Beuys exhibition needed to be rescheduled.[42] For reasons not known, Overby's European show never happened, so the Cirrus exhibition in November 1971 remained his only solo gallery show until 1975. According to Steve Kahn, Overby was "devastated" about the cancellations, but he continued to work on both of the major pieces cast at his brother's place, finishing them two days before the end of the year.

It is tempting to read much into a work that Overby also completed at the end of 1971. Poignantly titled *Shadow of Its Former Self*, 3 December 1971, it is made of latex rubber backed with cheesecloth. It is also separated by many "generations" from its original, which in fact was not the real garage door *Garage Door* was cast from, but a mold of it. During 1972 Overby made several more cast-latex pieces that address a variety of concerns. *Corner piece unlimited multiple*, 15 June 1972 (pl. 15), for example, investigates the conceptual implications of the "fragment" and the endless edition, while several doors—including *Blue slatted door*, 6 July 1972, and *Green screen door*, 10 July 1972 (pl. 14)—are almost like monochromatic paintings. Other, more idiosyncratic works from the same period are in fact "paintings"—for example, *Painting with 4 photos*, 12 July 1972, and

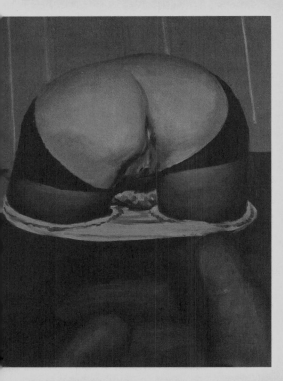

Figure 14
Dear Rear
1977
[cat. no. 60]

Three plywood sheets, 9 July 1972. All of these "signs" of painting were an indication that the work would soon change dramatically.

Hoping to create yet another temporal and material generation of the surfaces that still held his interest, Overby began sewing canvas "maps" of several of the earlier latex pieces, starting with the most recent, *Corner piece map*, 18 August 1972, and returning to others, like *Two window wall map*, 20 August 1972 (pl. 13). Effectively "slowing" down the photographic nature of the latex casts, the maps also have a conscientiousness in their fabrication that recalls the seemingly incongruous yet, for Overby, influential work of Franz Erhard Walther.[43] The precision of the maps also reinforced one of Overby's ongoing concerns, as he noted at the time: "significance may be that [a] map is usually accepted as reality."[44] Returning to New York in October, he produced a series of rubbings on paper: *N.Y. b&w rubbings*, 1–11 October 1972, and *N.Y. color rubbings*, 5–15 October 1972. In the context of the maps, they become ghosts, rapid materializations of the surfaces Overby never left. Another ghost appears in one of the first paintings he finished at the end of the year: in the middle of *Sky Plane*, 28 December 1972 (pl. 12), there is a barely perceptible outline of a square, which, for Overby, was "like finding a space in the clouds."[45]

. . .

In a review of a 1995 exhibition of Overby's early 1970s work at the Burnett Miller Gallery in Los Angeles—a show that included only fiberglass and latex casts, canvas maps, and neon work—Ina Blom, provoked just like Rimanelli and the rest of us by the red book, made Overby's (final) transition to (only) painting at the end of 1972 sound simultaneously scary and easy: "If latex had the capacity to render the world dead and limp, paint now seemed to take on the same quality, in much the same way that too much makeup makes a face look morbid rather than young, exposing lines rather than hiding them. . . . It is the transformation of paint with which we are today so thoroughly acquainted, the transformation in which paint is no longer a neutral colour substance, but able to convey concrete horror."[46] The evidence is clear that Overby understood such a transformation of *surface* even when he wasn't painting; the paintings that he produced between 1973 and 1978 are offered in this exhibition as final proof. Moreover, it is also clear that he had paintings like them substantially in mind while making all of the latex work: back in January 1970 he had extensively researched the techniques and materials of the old masters.

In January 1973 Overby finished what he considered to be one of his most important works, a painting descriptively yet provocatively titled *Dürer head on fake wood panel*, 15 January 1973 (pl. 11). One in a series of art historical "head" paintings from the time, it makes an issue of surface in terms of decay and disintegration and any attempts to hold

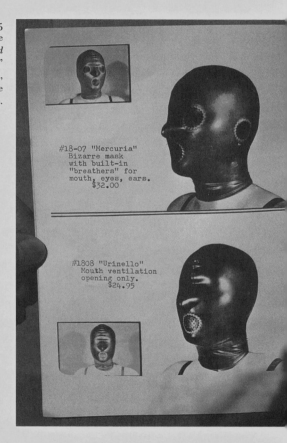

Figure 15
Overby's photograph of a page from *Exotic Rubber Wear and Acessories* [*sic*], a "Maggie May" catalogue (Cypress, Calif., August 1975), the image source for *Black Head*, 1975 (pl. 8).

them back—restoration, repainting, "replay." Conversely, *White wall with drawing*, 27 July 1973 (pl. 10), was, for Overby, an attempt to "put some humanity" back into minimalist painting, turning the formal structure of the doorway once again into a fig-urative presence.[47] (Other types of presence would become a big issue in 1974–75: he finished the red book in May 1974; he would move to Portland, Oregon, at the end of the year to return to design; and in June 1975 he would move to Santa Barbara, California, where he lived until 1982, when he returned to Los Angeles.)

Overby redirected the implications of the figurative back to yet another kind of damage in a deliberately troublesome "cutout" series of porno-graphic paintings made on the "bad" side of plywood. He showed several of these works, collectively called the ACX Series—including *Oh Annie* (pl. 9) and *Black Head* (pl. 8), both 1975—at the John Gunn Gallery in L.A. in October 1975. It is probably not surprising that they were not well received; Gunn was in fact faced with the same problem that John Weber had in 1971, but he chose to show the work anyway.[48] Overby based the ACX Series, as well as other paintings—like *Pink Head*, 1974–77 (pl. 6), and *Dear Rear*, 1977 (fig. 14)—upon images in bondage magazines (fig. 15). Their fetishizing functioned for him, strangely (even problematically), as "a symbol for a kind of man's repression of men."[49] Regardless of the fact that Overby cannot be completely "let off the hook" for these pictures, it is surely the case once again that he got the (tasteless) joke in depicting rubber this time

around, doing so in what can only be a "that's-so-funny-I-forgot-to-laugh" fashion.

At the same time, Overby returned to the "look" of design in paintings like *T-Zone*, 1977 (pl. 7), while also making sly references to things like flesh in *Apex Meat*, 1974–77 (pl. 5). He also turned a rubbing of a tile floor into a painting: *White Grid*, 1977 (pl. 4). A year later, in paintings like *Yellow Frag* (pl. 3) and *3 Line Painting* (pl. 1), both 1978, he returned the work to his "Baroque minimalism," as he put it, "stuffing it full of all kinds of things that one could get their hands on."[50] And, again, at the same time—as opposed to "finally," which by now we should know never existed for this artist—he brought "raw" material back to the work in a painting made of dry pigment, perfectly titled *Monster Blue*, 1978 (pl. 2).[51] What the paintings confirm, first, is that they are in fact mean-ingful "replays" of much of Overby's earlier work in other materials. At the same time, in the face of everything from failure to decay, from humor to hor-ror, they demonstrate the extent to which for Overby—and very likely for us too, in the end—the *parallel* itself will emerge as the one thing that never goes away.

NOTES

1. Walter Benjamin, "A Berlin Chronicle," in *Reflections: Essays, Aphorisms, Autobiographical Writings*, trans. Edmund Jephcott (New York: Schocken Books, 1986), 59.

2. Hillel Schwartz, *The Culture of the Copy: Striking Likenesses, Unreasonable Facsimiles* (New York: Zone Books, 1996), 319.

3. Michael Fried, "Art and Objecthood," *Artforum* 5 (June 1967): 23.

4. Steve Kahn, interview with the author, New York, 23 February 2000.

5. This essay merely scratches the surface of Overby's complicated and fascinating biography.

6. Anna C. Chave, "Minimalism and the Rhetoric of Power," *Arts Magazine* 64 (January 1990): 45.

7. Robert Overby, 1972 hand-bound sketchbook, 16 September 1972.

8. Sue Spaid, "Chipper: An Extended Life," self-published essay accompanying the exhibition *Robert Overby: Shadow of Its Former Self*, Sue Spaid Fine Art, Los Angeles, 7–31 July 1994, 4.

9. Cornelia H. Butler makes this point in "Ends and Means," in *Afterimage: Drawing through Process* (Los Angeles: Museum of Contemporary Art; Cambridge: MIT Press, 1999), 109 n. 42.

10. These slides, which were prepared in July 1970, are in Overby's slide archive.

11. David Rimanelli, "Robert Overby," *Artforum* 36 (April 1997): 83.

12. Marty Neumeier, "Robert Overby," *Communication Arts* 20 (January–February 1979): 38.

13. Dorfsman to Overby, 1 July 1969, in Overby's correspondence files.

14. Letter of agreement from Overby to Arnoldi, 6 September 1969, in Overby's correspondence files.

15. The entire collection is recorded in a document with the title "CBS Studio Center Catalog of Art Objects," in Overby's archive.

16. Overby mentions Dick Bell to Peter Clothier in a series of extensive, invaluable, and unpublished interviews that were recorded on nine cassette tapes between 28 January and 19 May 1986 (tape 3, 3 February 1986).

17. Clothier interview, tape 3, 3 February 1986. The whereabouts of the artworks by Overby that were sold to CBS in 1969 are currently unknown.

18. Clothier interview, tape 5, 10 March 1986.

19. Clothier interview, tape 3, 3 February 1986.

20. Overby, 1970 hand-bound sketchbook, 7 March 1970.

21. Overby, 1970 hand-bound sketchbook, 5 May 1970.

22. My speculations here are based largely upon two meetings that I had with Overby in the fall of 1992, as well as several conversations with Linda Burnham, a painter who was married to him from 1980 until his death in 1993.

23. Clothier interview, tape 6, 8 April 1986.

24. Clothier interview, tape 5, 10 March 1986.

25. Clothier interview, tape 8, n.d.

26. Michael Duncan, "Ruins and Replicas," *Art in America* 84 (July 1996): 79.

27. Overby, 1972 hand-bound sketchbook, 1 July 1972.

28. Overby, 1971 hand-bound sketchbook, 20 January 1971.

29. Clothier interview, tape 7, 15 April 1986.

30. Overby to Elizabeth Clark, 20 July 1972, in Overby's correspondence files.

31. William Wilson, "Art Walk: A Critical Guide to the Galleries," *Los Angeles Times*, 24 December 1971.

32. The pictures were actually prints of black-and-white photographs taken by Steve Kahn, many of which would end up in the red book.

33. There are various notes in Overby's 1971 sketchbook concerning the shipping of work to New York and Europe.

34. In the Clothier interviews, Overby makes it clear that he was not represented by Cirrus (tape 6, 8 April 1986).

35. Susan Stewart, *Crimes of Writing: Problems in the Containment of Representation* (Durham, N.C.: Duke University Press, 1994), 274.

36. Rimanelli, "Robert Overby," 83.

37. Overby did a drawing on October 17 of the gallery's floor plan in his 1971 hand-bound sketchbook, indicating that he was thinking about showing the following works from the Barclay House Series: *103 (test), Barclay House; Small wall with slats, first floor; Tone-bar door, first floor; Sun room with window, second floor; Cabinet with door, second floor; Drawer door, second floor; South door, third floor.*

38. Clothier interview, tape 8, n.d. Overby also reveals that a burglar broke into the room while the piece was being made, breaking a window and cutting through the latex membrane: "When he got inside he was in a creepy, closed room. A rubber room! I don't know what he thought."

39. Weber to Overby, 15 December 1971, in Overby's correspondence files. It is important to know that Overby stayed on good terms with the dealer, corresponding with him on more than one occasion.

40. Clothier interview, tape 7, 8 April 1986.

41. Kushner to Overby, 6 June 1972, in Overby's correspondence files.

42. Amelio to Overby, 3 November 1971, in Overby's correspondence files.

43. According to Linda Burnham, one of Overby's prized possessions was a book on Walther's work: Adriani Götz, *Franz Erhard Walther: Werkmonographie* (Cologne: M. DuMont Schauberg, 1972). Overby sewed canvas bags to hold each of his maps, something that very likely was provoked by Walther's production in the 1970s. Moreover, the book also included a few reproductions of drawings done by Walther in 1957, highly designed images of such things as the word *Afrika*, and a package of "XOX" biscuits.

44. Overby, 1972 hand-bound sketchbook, 31 July 1972.

45. Clothier interview, tape 9, 19 May 1986.

46. Ina Blom, "Robert Overby," *Frieze*, no. 28 (May 1996): 67.

47. Clothier interview, tape 9, 19 May 1986.

48. Gunn to Overby, 10 October 1975, in Overby's correspondence files.

49. Clothier interview, tape 9, 19 May 1986.

50. Ibid.

51. In November 1979 Overby exhibited a series of small, square, monochromatic pigment paintings in the entrance gallery of the Los Angeles Institute of Contemporary Art. They are even more fragile and unstable than *Monster Blue*.

Checklist of the Exhibition

Note to the reader: Works from 1969 to 1973 are listed according to the order in which they appear (in reverse chronological order, with occasional exceptions) in the artist's privately published catalogue, *Robert Overby: 336 to 1, August 1973–July 1969* (Los Angeles, 1974); works from 1974 to 1978 are listed in the order indicated in the archives of the artist.

1. *Space No. 9 (study for RTO)*
August 1969
Serigraph
Edition of 9
66 x 50.8 cm (26 x 20 in.)
Estate of Robert Overby

2. *Five Components in regular and exploded views*
September 1969
Serigraph
Two panels, 33 x 33 cm (13 x 13 in.) each
Estate of Robert Overby

3. *Great American Pepper*
September 1969
Serigraph
Edition of 10 in various color combinations
60 x 43.8 cm ($23^5/8$ x $17^1/4$ in.)
Estate of Robert Overby

4. *Adhesium*
October 1969
Serigraph
Edition of 18
50.8 x 44.5 cm (20 x $17^1/2$ in.)
Estate of Robert Overby
[Plate 42]

5. *Tan and Blue Stretch*
8 July 1970
Polyvinyl chloride and resin
102.9 x 154.9 x 7.6 cm ($40^1/2$ x 61 x 3 in.)
Estate of Robert Overby
[Plate 41]

6. *Sky-Hi*
14 July 1970
Polyvinyl chloride and resin
137.2 x 121.9 cm (54 x 48 in.)
Collection of Joe Fronek
[Plate 40]

7. *Large Yellow and Silver Stretch*
16 July 1970
Polyvinyl chloride and resin
149.9 x 205.7 x 7.6 cm (59 x 81 x 3 in.)
Estate of Robert Overby

8. *Stephanie's Sox*
1 August 1970
Graphite, marker, and watercolor on paper
50.8 x 61 cm (20 x 24 in.)
Estate of Robert Overby

9. *Stephanie's Sox are Blue*
1 August 1970
Graphite, marker, and watercolor on paper
43.8 x 43.8 cm ($17^1/4$ x $17^1/4$ in.)
Estate of Robert Overby

10. *Trilobite*
20 September 1970
Multilayered resins
4.1 x 9.8 x 13.3 cm ($1^5/8$ x $3^7/8$ x $5^1/4$ in.)
Private collection, Los Angeles

11. *Monkey Grip*
20 September 1970
Nickel-plated resin
3.5 x 9.2 x 6 cm ($1^3/8$ x $3^5/8$ x $2^3/8$ in.)
Collection of Tom Knechtel
[Figure 8]

12. *Lizard Soup No. 2*
20 September 1970
Cadmium-plated resin and acrylic
9.5 x 9.5 x 10.2 cm ($3^3/4$ x $3^3/4$ x 4 in.)
Estate of Robert Overby
[Plate 38]

13. *Madonna Door*
5 October 1970
Polyvinyl chloride
213.4 x 71.1 x 27.9 cm (84 x 28 x 11 in.)
Estate of Robert Overby
[Plate 37]

14. *Concrete screen doors*
9 October 1970–22 January 1971
Concrete and steel
Edition of 5
203.2 x 114.3 x 12.7 cm
(80 x 45 x 5 in.) each
Estate of Robert Overby
[Plate 36]

15. *Projected space between my legs*
16 October 1970
Concrete and steel
Edition of 3
Thin one: 115.6 x 17.8 x 5.1 cm
($45^1/2$ x 7 x 2 in.)

Base point left: 111.8 x 24.1 x 5.1 cm
(44 x 9^{1}/$_{2}$ x 2 in.)
Base point right: 111.1 x 21.6 x 4.4 cm
(43^{3}/$_{4}$ x 8^{1}/$_{2}$ x 1^{3}/$_{4}$ in.)
Estate of Robert Overby
[Plate 35]

16. *50 painting sketches* (selection)
8 April 1970–16 November 1972
Gouache and pencil on paper
Miscellaneous sizes
Estate of Robert Overby

17. *R.M. Rill*
7 February 1971
Lead
5.1 x 20.3 cm (2 x 8 in.)
Private collection, Los Angeles
[Plate 34]

18. *Rubber sock*
18 February 1971
Cast rubber
30.5 x 20.3 cm (12 x 8 in.)
Estate of Robert Overby

19. *Door edge*
19 February 1971
Polyester resin and fiberglass
203.2 x 5.1 x 4.4 cm (80 x 2 x 1^{3}/$_{4}$ in.)
Collection of Tony and Gail Ganz

20. *Opaque door edge*
24 February 1971
Polyester resin, fiberglass, and
acrylic lacquer
203.2 x 5.1 x 4.4 cm (80 x 2 x 1^{3}/$_{4}$ in.)
Private collection
[Plate 33]

21. *Concrete screen door with hole*
20 February 1971
Concrete and steel
Two parts, 203.2 x 114.3 x 12.7 cm
(80 x 45 x 5 in.) overall
Private collection, Los Angeles

22. *Concrete screen door handle*
20 February 1971
Concrete and steel
28.6 x 15.9 x 7.6 cm (11^{1}/$_{4}$ x 6^{1}/$_{4}$ x 3 in.)
Collection of Steve Kahn, New York
[Plate 32]

23. *Blue screen door*
11 March 1971
Polyester resin and fiberglass
194.3 x 80.6 x 3.8 cm
(76^{1}/$_{2}$ x 31^{3}/$_{4}$ x 1^{1}/$_{2}$ in.)
Collection of Linda Burnham, Glendale,
California
[Plate 31]

24. *Garage Door*
13 May 1971
Latex rubber
213.4 x 121.9 cm (84 x 48 in.)
Collection of Arlene and Barry Hockfield,
Pennsylvania
[Plate 30]

25. *15°*
2 June 1971
Latex rubber
Two parts, 914.4 x 16.5 cm (360 x 6^{1}/$_{2}$ in.)
and 824.2 x 16.5 cm (324^{1}/$_{2}$ x 6^{1}/$_{2}$ in.)
Collection of Tony and Gail Ganz
[Figure 12]

26. *Hall painting, first floor*
From the Barclay House Series
4 August 1971
Latex rubber
273.1 x 198.1 cm (107^{1}/$_{2}$ x 78 in.)
Estate of Robert Overby

27. *Drawer door, second floor*
From the Barclay House Series
4 August 1971
Latex rubber
18.4 x 38.7 cm (7^{1}/$_{4}$ x 15^{1}/$_{4}$ in.)
Estate of Robert Overby

28. *Door with hole, second floor*
From the Barclay House Series
4 August 1971
Latex rubber
204.5 x 86.4 cm (80^{1}/$_{2}$ x 34 in.)
Collection of Joe Barron, New York
[Plate 29]

29. *North hall wall, second floor*
From the Barclay House Series
4 August 1971
Latex rubber
279.4 x 955 cm (110 x 376 in.)
Estate of Robert Overby
[Plate 28]

30. *Door without center panel, third floor*
From the Barclay House Series
4 August 1971
Latex rubber
201.9 x 83.8 cm (79^{1}/$_{2}$ x 33 in.)
Collection of Barry Sloane, Los Angeles
[Plate 27]

31. *Paul's door, third floor*
From the Barclay House Series
4 August 1971
Latex rubber
210.8 x 119.4 x 12.7 cm (83 x 47 x 5 in.)
Collection of Whitney Museum of
American Art. Promised gift of
Norman Dubrow, P.5.96
[Plate 26]

32. *South door, third floor*
From the Barclay House Series
4 August 1971
Latex rubber
209.6 x 100.3 cm (82$^{1}/_{2}$ x 39$^{1}/_{2}$ in.)
Estate of Robert Overby

33. *East hall wall, third floor (Grey wall)*
From the Barclay House Series
4 August 1971
Latex rubber
264.2 x 473.7 cm (104 x 186$^{1}/_{2}$ in.)
Estate of Robert Overby
[Plate 25]

34. *Closet doors, third floor*
From the Barclay House Series
4 August 1971
Latex rubber
265.4 x 160 cm (104$^{1}/_{2}$ x 63 in.)
Estate of Robert Overby
[Plate 24]

35. *East room with 2 windows, third floor*
From the Barclay House Series
4 August 1971
Latex rubber
273.1 x 442 cm (107$^{1}/_{2}$ x 174 in.)
Estate of Robert Overby
[Plate 23]

36. *West hall painting, third floor*
From the Barclay House Series
4 August 1971
Latex rubber
189.9 x 213.4 cm (74$^{3}/_{4}$ x 84 in.)
Collection of Susan and Barry Sussman

37. *Scotch tape painting, third floor*
From the Barclay House Series
4 August 1971
Latex rubber
127 x 165.7 cm (50 x 65$^{1}/_{4}$ in.)
Estate of Robert Overby
[Plate 22]

38. *Long wall, third floor*
From the Barclay House Series
4 August 1971
Latex rubber
269.2 x 584.2 cm (106 x 230 in.)
Estate of Robert Overby
[Plate 21]

39. *Colored room wall, third floor*
From the Barclay House Series
4 August 1971
Latex rubber
265.4 x 388.6 cm (104$^{1}/_{2}$ x 153 in.)
Estate of Robert Overby

40. *Blue door edge*
8 April 1971
Neon
Height: 203.2 cm (80 in.)
Estate of Robert Overby
[Plate 20]

41. *Gas can orange*
15 December 1971
Latex rubber
38.7 x 29.5 cm (15$^{1}/_{4}$ x 11$^{5}/_{8}$ in.)
Collection of Jeff Kerns, Los Angeles

42. *Light meters, Paul's place*
16 December 1971
Latex rubber
25.4 x 47 x 25.4 cm (10 x 18$^{1}/_{2}$ x 10 in.)
Estate of Robert Overby
[Plate 19]

43. *Living room, Paul's place*
29 December 1971
Latex rubber
240.3 x 344.2 x 353.1 cm
(94$^{5}/_{8}$ x 135$^{1}/_{2}$ x 139 in.)
Estate of Robert Overby
[Plates 17, 18]

44. *Stairwell, Paul's place*
29 December 1971
Latex rubber
254 x 360.7 x 78.7 cm (100 x 142 x 31 in.)
Estate of Robert Overby
[Plate 16, figure 13]

45. *Corner piece unlimited multiple*
15 June 1972
Latex rubber
71.1 x 61 x 40.6 cm (28 x 24 x 16 in.)
Collection of Kenneth L. Freed, Boston
[Plate 15]

46. *Blue slatted door*
6 July 1972
Latex rubber
198.8 x 60.3 cm (78^{1}/$_{4}$ x 23^{3}/$_{4}$ in.)
Estate of Robert Overby

47. *Three plywood sheets* (selection)
9 July 1972
Latex rubber
119.4 x 167.6 cm (47 x 66 in.) each
Estate of Robert Overby

48. *Green screen door*
10 July 1972
Latex rubber with metal handle and hinge
203.2 x 75.6 cm (80 x 29^{3}/$_{4}$ in.)
Collection of John Robertshaw, New York
[Plate 14]

49. *Green door with small window*
11 July 1972
Latex rubber
205.1 x 142.2 cm (80^{3}/$_{4}$ x 56 in.)
Collection of Leonard Hirshan
[Plate 28]

50. *Painting with 4 photos*
12 July 1972
Latex rubber and photos
58.4 x 71.8 cm (23 x 28^{1}/$_{4}$ in.)
Estate of Robert Overby

51. *Corner piece map*
18 August 1972
Canvas
61 x 48.3 x 38.1 cm (24 x 19 x 15 in.)
Collection of Kenneth L. Freed, Boston

52. *Two window wall map*
20 August 1972
Canvas
268 x 406.4 cm (105^{1}/$_{2}$ x 160 in.)
Estate of Robert Overby
[Plate 13]

53. *Tone-bar door map*
21 August 1972
Canvas
198.1 x 76.2 cm (78 x 30 in.)
Private collection, courtesy Fredericks
Freiser Gallery, New York
[Figure 7]

54. *Sky Plane*
28 December 1972
Oil on canvas
36.2 x 45.7 cm (14^{1}/$_{4}$ x 18 in.)
Collection of Dean Valentine and Amy
Adelson, Los Angeles
[Plate 12]

55. *Dürer head on fake wood panel*
15 January 1973
Oil on canvas
35.6 x 27.9 cm (14 x 11 in.)
Collection of Tom Lazarus, Los Angeles
[Plate 11]

56. *TV test pattern*
16 February 1973
Latex rubber
33.7 x 40 cm (13^{1}/$_{4}$ x 15^{3}/$_{4}$ in.)
Estate of Robert Overby

57. *White wall with drawing*
27 July 1973
Oil on canvas
63.5 x 96.5 cm (25 x 38 in.)
Estate of Robert Overby
[Plate 10]

58. *Oh Annie*
1975
Oil on plywood
233.7 x 119.4 cm (92 x 47 in.)
Estate of Robert Overby, courtesy Fredericks
Freiser Gallery, New York
[Plate 9]

59. *Black Head*
1975
Oil on plywood
115.6 x 85.1 cm (45^{1}/$_{2}$ x 33^{1}/$_{2}$ in.)
Collection of Charlotte and Paul Corddry,
New York
[Plate 8]

60. *Dear Rear*
1977
Oil on canvas
26.7 x 20.3 cm (10^{1}/$_{2}$ x 8 in.)
Collection of Lari Pittman and Roy Dowell
[Figure 14]

61. *T-Zone*
1977
Oil on canvas
61 x 45.7 cm (24 x 18 in.)
Estate of Robert Overby
[Plate 7]

62. *Pink Head*
1974–77
Oil on canvas
91.4 x 73.7 cm (36 x 29 in.)
Estate of Robert Overby, courtesy
Fredericks Freiser Gallery, New York
[Plate 6]

63. *Apex Meat*
1974–77
Oil on canvas
127 x 127 cm (50 x 50 in.)
Estate of Robert Overby
[Plate 5]

64. *White Grid*
1977
Oil on canvas
269.2 x 219.7 cm (106 x 86^1/2 in.)
Estate of Robert Overby
[Plate 4]

65. *Yellow Frag*
1978
Oil on canvas
40.6 x 34.3 cm (16 x 13^1/2 in.)
Collection of Linda Burnham, Glendale,
California
[Plate 3]

66. *Monster Blue*
1978
Dry pigment
152.4 x 137.2 cm (60 x 54 in.)
Private collection, Los Angeles
[Plate 2]

67. *3 Line Painting*
1978
Oil on canvas
121.9 x 121.9 cm (48 x 48 in.)
Collection of Marty Neumeier, Palo Alto,
California
[Plate 1]

68. *Robert Overby's sketchbooks*
1969–74
Estate of Robert Overby

Exhibition History and Bibliography

Robert Overby
Born 1935, Harvey, Illinois
Died 1993, Los Angeles

Education
1953–54, 1956–57
    School of the Art Institute of Chicago
1958–59
    Art Center School, Los Angeles
1970
    B.A., Chouinard Art Institute, Los Angeles

Solo Exhibitions
1969
    Chouinard Gallery, Los Angeles
1971
    Odds and Ends, Chouinard Gallery, Los Angeles
    Around the House and Across the Street, Cirrus Gallery, Los Angeles
1975
    ACX, John Gunn Gallery, Los Angeles
1979
    Los Angeles Institute of Contemporary Art, Los Angeles
1989
    Jan Baum Gallery, Los Angeles
1994
    Shadow of Its Former Self, Sue Spaid Fine Art, Los Angeles
1995
    Burnett Miller Gallery, Los Angeles

1996
Robert Overby, 1971–1985, Jessica Fredericks Gallery, New York
1998
The Barclay House, Jessica Fredericks Gallery, New York

Group Exhibitions
1971
Opening 420 Building, John Weber Gallery, New York
John Weber Gallery, New York
1975
Group Show, Prints on Broxton, Los Angeles
1979
Santa Barbara Artists Invitational, Santa Barbara Arts Council, Santa Barbara
1996
The Palace of Good Luck: Sam Durant, Toland Grinnell, Zuzanna Janin, Robert Overby, Glen Seator, Kent Young, Burnett Miller Gallery, Los Angeles
1997
Scene of the Crime, UCLA at the Armand Hammer Museum of Art and Cultural Center, Los Angeles (curated by Ralph Rugoff, catalogue)
1998
Rubber, Robert Miller Gallery, New York (curated by Anna O'Sullivan)
1999
Surface <=> Structure, Peggy Phelps Gallery and East Gallery, Claremont Graduate University, Claremont, California (curated by Sue Spaid, catalogue)
Afterimage: Drawing through Process, Museum of Contemporary Art, Los Angeles (curated by Cornelia H. Butler, catalogue)

Bibliography

1971

William Wilson, "A Critical Guide to the Galleries," *Los Angeles Times*,
24 December 1971, pt. 2.

1979

Marty Neumeier, "Robert Overby," *Communication Arts* 20 (January–February
1979): 32–42.

1989

Suvan Geer, "Robert Overby," *Los Angeles Times*, 15 September 1989.

1994

Sue Spaid, "Chipper: An Extended Life," essay accompanying exhibition *Robert
Overby: Shadow of Its Former Self*, Sue Spaid Fine Art, Los Angeles, July 1994.

David Pagel, "The Unusual World of Robert Overby," *Los Angeles Times*, 14 July
1994, sec. F.

Peter Frank, "Art Picks of the Week: Robert Overby, O'Keeffe-Slawson-Wallin,"
LA Weekly, 22–28 July 1994, 120.

Terry R. Myers, "Robert Overby," *Art Issues*, no. 34 (September–October 1994):
46.

1995

David Pagel, "The Dark Side," *Los Angeles Times*, 12 October 1995.

Peter Frank, "Art Picks of the Week: Robert Overby, Linda Burnham, and Lewis
DeSoto," *LA Weekly*, 27 October–2 November 1995, 150.

1996

Peter Frank, "Robert Overby," *Art News* 95 (March 1996): 119–20.

Ina Blom, "Robert Overby," *Frieze*, no. 28 (May 1996): 66–67.

Michael Duncan, "Ruins and Replicas," *Art in America* 84 (July 1996): 76–79.

David Pagel, "Lots of Luck," *Los Angeles Times*, 25 July 1996, sec. F.